SCHOLASTIC

FIRST HOME

NUMBERS

60+ Age-Perfect Reproducibles That Help Youngsters Learn Their Numbers From 1 to 30

by Alyse Sweeney

NEW YORK • TORONTO • LONDON • AUCKLAND • SYDNEY
MEXICO CITY • NEW DELHI • HONG KONG • BUENOS AIRES

Teaching *Resources*

Edited by Elizabeth Bennett
Cover design by Brian LaRossa
Cover Illustraion by Peggy Tagel
Interior design by Brian LaRossa

ISBN-13: 978-0-545-15043-9
ISBN-10: 0-545-15043-4

3 4 5 6 7 8 9 10   40   15 14 13 12 11 10

TABLE OF CONTENTS

INTRODUCTION

First Homework: Numbers is filled with fun reproducible send-home pages that reinforce students' classroom learning.

Over the past decade, research has suggested that homework helps children develop skills and build study habits. Homework also fosters independence and responsibility—just what little ones crave! The letter to parents on page 5 includes a rationale for homework and tips for creating a positive homework environment.

First Homework is designed with a predictable format to encourage student independence and feelings of success. Review pages throughout the book further support learning. A variety of engaging activities for numbers 1 through 30 and 100 include:

- Tracing and writing numbers
- Counting objects in a set
- Drawing specified quantities
- Identifying numbers
- Sequencing numbers

First Homework: Numbers helps both teachers and parents accompany children down the thrilling road of learning and mastery.

—The Editors

FIRST HOMEWORK: NUMBERS meets these important NCTM* Standards.

- Count with understanding and recognize "how many" in sets of objects
- Develop a sense of whole numbers and represent and use them in flexible ways
- Connect number words and numerals to the quantities they represent

*National Council of Teachers of Mathematics

Dear Parents,

This year, your child will bring home reproducible homework pages from Scholastic's **First Homework: Numbers** book. These homework pages reinforce our classroom learning of number recognition, number formation, quantities, and counting. Homework provides children with practice while fostering independence and responsibility—just what little ones crave!

As your child is new to homework, I'd like to share four ways to create a positive homework environment, from the Office of Educational Research and Improvement.

1. Show that you think homework is important. Provide a consistent time and place for it and turn off the television.

2. Offer help when needed, but let your child do as much as he or she can independently.

3. Check your child's work.

4. Talk to me if your child struggles with homework.

Homework is a great way to bring home and school closer together. Have fun watching your child grow and learn with these **First Homework** pages.

Sincerely,

_____

I

Name _____

I one

Trace and write.

Color each set of I.

Name _____

1 one

Draw 1 crab.

Color each crab with the number 1.

Write the missing number.

_____ 2 3

Name

2 two

Trace and write.

Color each set of 2.

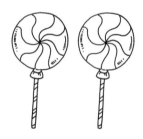
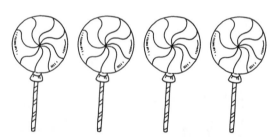
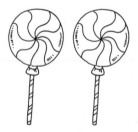

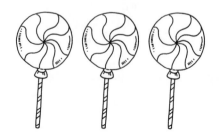

Name _____

2 two

Draw 2 lollipops.

Color each lollipop with the number 2.

Write the missing number.

1 _____ 3

3

Name _____

3 three

Trace and write.

Color each set of 3.

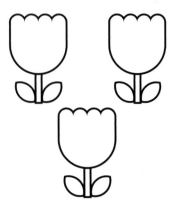
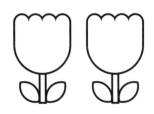

Name

3 three

Draw 3 flowers.

Color each flower with the number 3.

Write the missing number.

2 _____ 4

4

Name _____

4 four

Trace and write.

Color each set of 4.

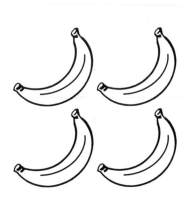

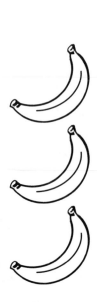

Name

4 four

Draw 4 bananas.

Color each banana with the number 4.

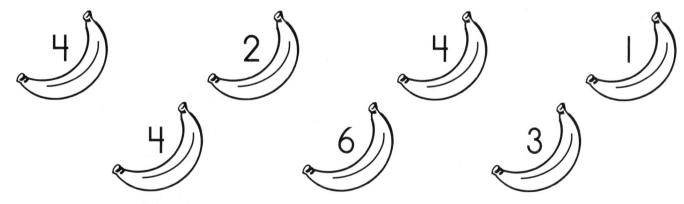

Write the missing number.

3 ___ 5

Name _____

5 five

Trace and write.

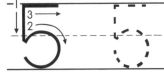

Color each nest with 5 eggs.

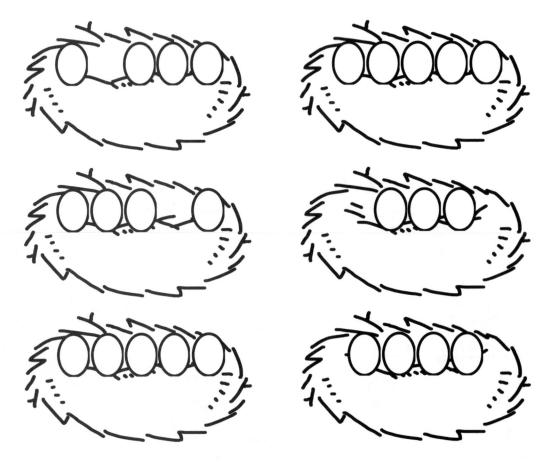

Name _____

5 five

Draw 5 eggs.

Color each egg with the number 5.

Write the missing number.

4 _____ 6

6

Name _____

6 six

Trace and write.

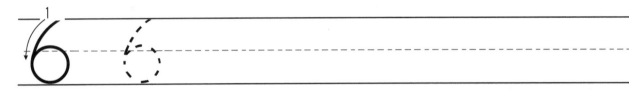

Color each set of 6.

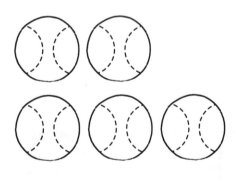

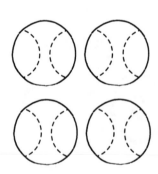

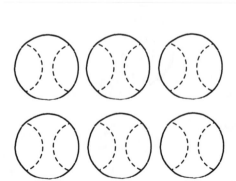

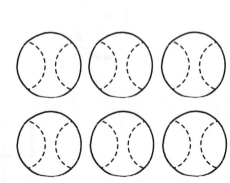

Name _____

6 six

Draw 6 balls.

Color each ball with the number 6.

Write the missing number.

7

7 seven

Trace and write.

7 7̸

Color each set of 7.

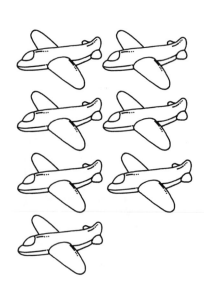

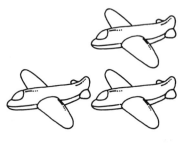

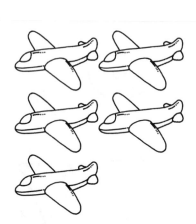

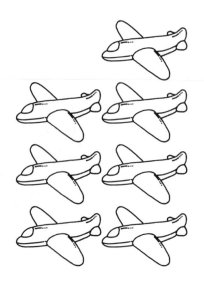

Name

7 seven

Draw 7 planes.

Color each plane with the number 7.

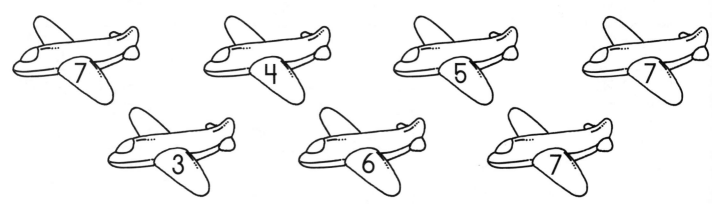

Write the missing number.

6 ____ 8

Name _____

8 eight

Trace and write.

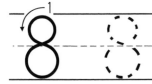

Color the set of 8 houses.

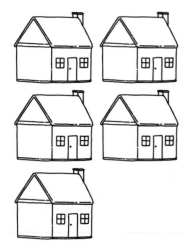

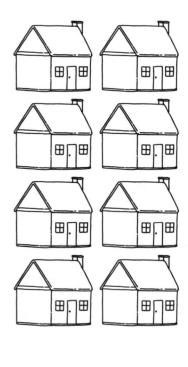

Name

8 eight

Draw 8 houses.

Color each house with the number 8.

8   7   9   1

8   6   8

Write the missing number.

7 _____ 9

Name

q nine

Trace and write.

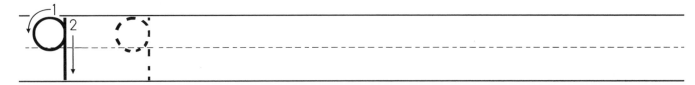

Color the tree with q apples.

Name _____

q nine

Draw q apples.

Color each apple with the number q.

Write the missing number.

8 ____ 10

10

Name _____

10 ten

Trace and write.

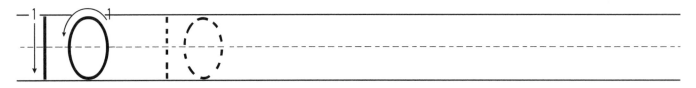

Color the pizza with 10 pepperonis.

Name _____

10 ten

Draw 10 pizzas.

Color each pizza with the number 10.

Write the missing number.

Name _____

Draw a path inside each number.

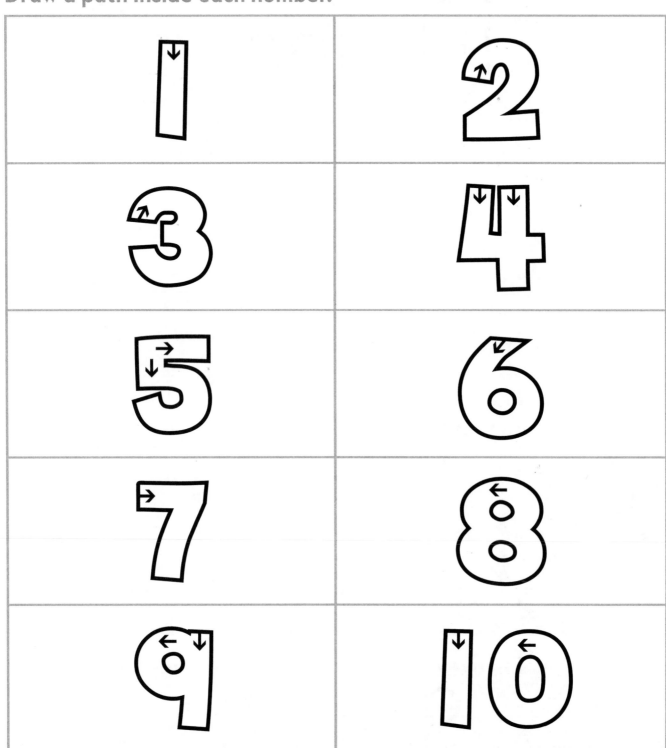

Name _____

Connect the numbers 1–10 to make a picture. Color the picture.

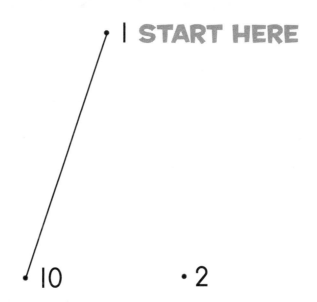

•9

•7

•5

Name

11 eleven

Trace and write.

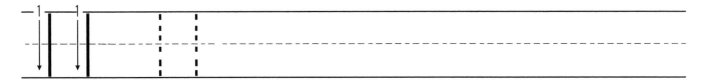

Color the snakes with 11 stripes.

Name _____

11 eleven

Draw a line from the 11 to each snake with an 11.

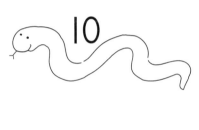
10

1

12

11

11

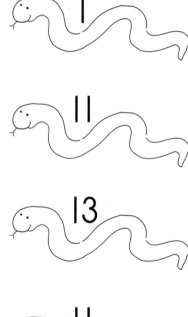
1

11

13

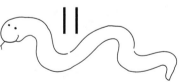
11

Write the missing number.

10 _____ 12

12

12 twelve

Trace and write.

Color the set of 12.

Name _____

12 twelve

Draw a line from the 12 to each cupcake with a 12.

Write the missing number.

11 _____ 13

Name _____

13   thirteen

Trace and write.

Color the watermelon with 13 seeds.

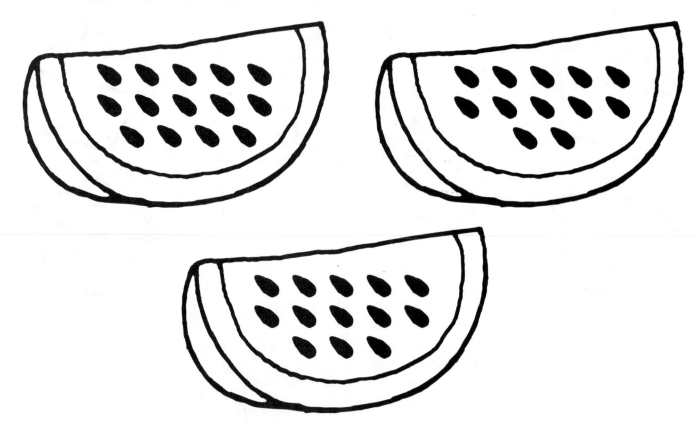

Name

13 thirteen

Draw a line from the 13 to each watermelon slice with a 13.

Write the missing number.

12 _____ 14

Name _____

14 fourteen

Trace and write.

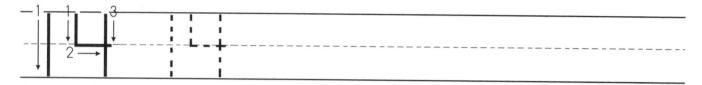

Color the set of 14.

Name _____

14 fourteen

Draw a line from the 14 to each heart with a 14.

Write the missing number.

13 _____ 15

Name

15 fifteen

Trace and write.

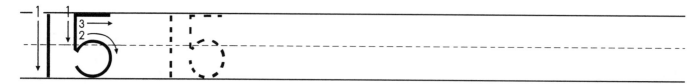

Color the bathtub with 15 bubbles.

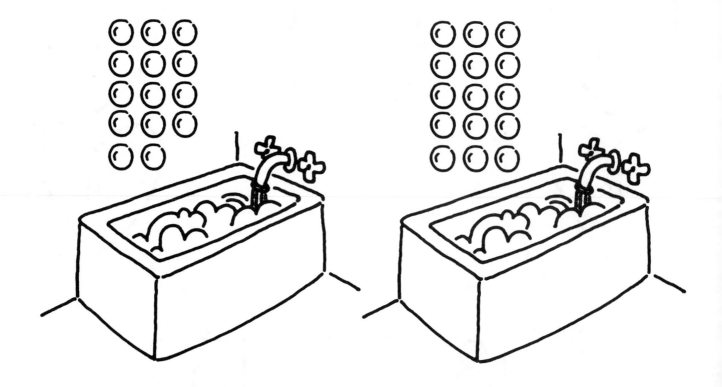

Name _____

15 fifteen

Draw a line from the 15 to each bubble with a 15.

Write the missing number.

14 _____ 16

Name _____

16 sixteen

Trace and write.

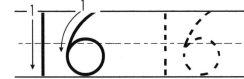

Color the cloud with 16 raindrops.

Name _____

16 sixteen

Draw a line from the 16 to each cloud with a 16.

Write the missing number.

15 _____ 17

Name _____

17 seventeen

Trace and write.

Color the set of 17.

Name _____

17 seventeen

Draw a line from the 17 to each fish with a 17.

Write the missing number.

16 _____ 18

18

Name _____

18 eighteen

Trace and write.

Color the set of 18.

Name _____

18 eighteen

Draw a line from the 18 to each shoe with an 18.

Write the missing number.

17 _____ 19

Name _____

19 nineteen

Trace and write.

Color the set of 19.

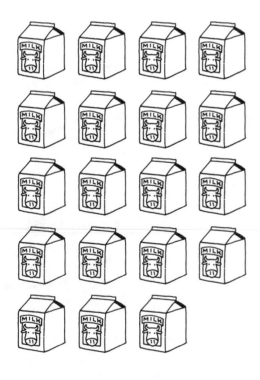

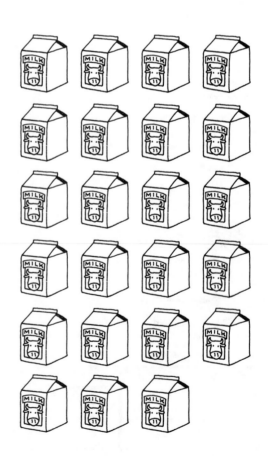

Name _____

19 nineteen

Draw a line from the 19 to each milk carton with a 19.

Write the missing number.

18 _____ 20

Name _____

20 twenty

Trace and write.

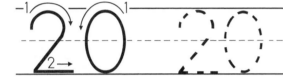

Color each set of **20**.

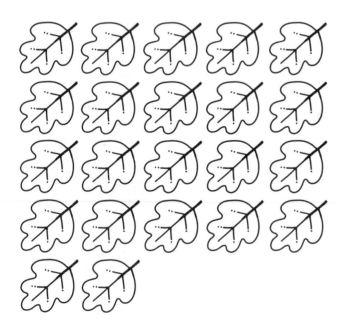
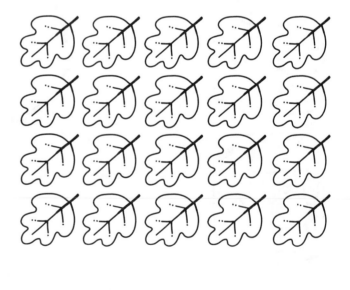

Name

20 twenty

Draw a line from the 20 to each leaf with a 20.

Write the missing number.

19 _____ 21

Name _____

Draw a path inside each number.

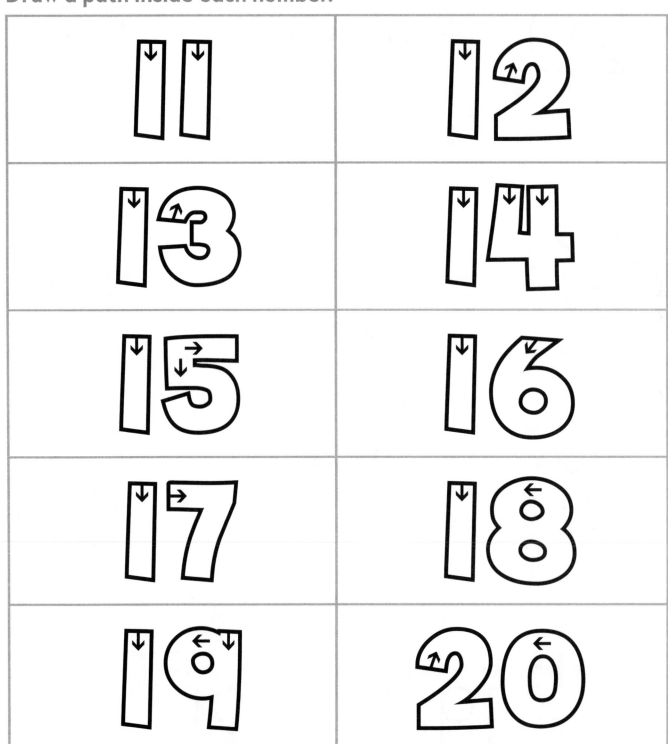

Name

Connect the numbers 11–20 to make a picture. Color the picture.

• 11 **START HERE**

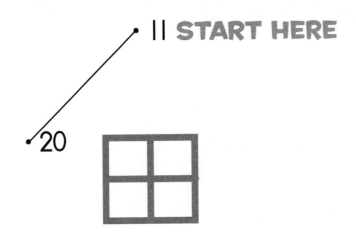

• 20

• 19

• 12

• 16

• 15

• 18

• 17

• 14

• 13

Name _____

21   twenty-one

Draw a path inside the numbers.

Color each circle with a 21.

 21   22   21   24

11   25   21   21

Name _____

21 twenty-one

Draw a path for the car to follow.  at 21.

1 2 3 4 5 6 7 8 9 10 11 12

13

14

21 20 19 18 17 16 15

22

23 24 25 26 27 28 29 30

Write the missing number.

20 _____ 22

Name _____

22 twenty-two

Draw a path inside the numbers.

Color each triangle with a 22.

 22

26

 26

12

 22

25

24

22

Name

22 twenty-two

Draw a path for the car to follow.  at 22.

1 2 3 4 5 6 7 8 9 10 11 12

13

20 19 18 17 16 15 14

21

22

23 24 25 26 27 28 29 30

Write the missing number.

21 _____ 23

Name _____

23 twenty-three

Draw a path inside the numbers.

Color each square with a 23.

23		26		25		26
	27		23		25	13

Name

23 twenty-three

Draw a path for the car to follow.  at 23.

1 2 3 4 5 6 7 8 9 10 11 12

13

14

21 20 19 18 17 16 15

22

23 24 25 26 27 28 29 30

Write the missing number.

22 _____ 24

Name _____

24 twenty-four

Draw a path inside the numbers.

Color each oval with a 24.

26   24   14   26

27   25   24   21

Name _____

24 twenty-four

Draw a path for the car to follow.  at 24.

 1 2 3 4 5 6 7 8 9 10 11 12
13
14
21 20 19 18 17 16 15
22
23 24 25 26 27 28 29 30

Write the missing number.

23 _____ 25

Name _____

25　twenty-five　

Draw a path inside the numbers.

Color each diamond with a 25.

25　27　26　25　15　25　26　22

Name _____

25 twenty-five

Draw a path for the car to follow. **at 25.**

1 2 3 4 5 6 7 8 9 10 11 12

13

14

21 20 19 18 17 16 15

22

23 24 25 26 27 28 29 30

Write the missing number.

24 _____ 26

Name _____

26 twenty-six

Draw a path inside the numbers.

Color each rectangle with a 26.

25   26   15   26

   27   25   25   22

Name

26 twenty-six

Draw a path for the car to follow. at 26.

1 2 3 4 5 6 7 8 9 10 11 12 13 14

21 20 19 18 17 16 15

22

23 24 25 26 27 28 29 30

Write the missing number.

25 _____ 27

Name _____

27 twenty–seven

Draw a path inside the numbers.

Color each arrow with a 27.

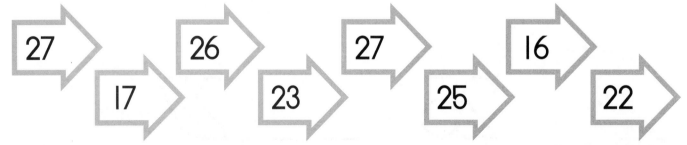

Name _____

27 twenty-seven

Draw a path for the car to follow.  at 27.

1 2 3 4 5 6 7 8 9 10 11 12 13 14

21 20 19 18 17 16 15

22

23 24 25 26 27 28 29 30

Write the missing number.

26 ____ 28

Name _____

28 twenty-eight

Draw a path inside the numbers.

Color each heart with a 28.

Name _____

28 twenty-eight

Draw a path for the car to follow. **STOP** at 28.

1 2 3 4 5 6 7 8 9 10 11 12

13

14

21 20 19 18 17 16 15

22

23 24 25 26 27 28 29 30

Write the missing number.

27 _____ 29

Name _____

29 twenty-nine

Draw a path inside the numbers.

Color each star with a 29.

19   26   29   26

29   28   25   29

Name _____

29 twenty-nine

Draw a path for the car to follow. at 29.

 1 2 3 4 5 6 7 8 9 10 11 12 13 14

21 20 19 18 17 16 15

22

23 24 25 26 27 28 29 30

Write the missing number.

28 _____ 30

Name _____

30   thirty

Draw a path inside the numbers.

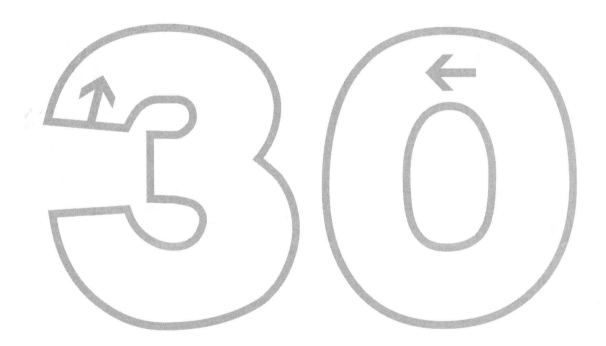

Color each stop sign with a 30.

30 33 31 32

20 10 30 30

Name _____

30 thirty

Draw a path for the car to follow.  at 30.

1 2 3 4 5 6 7 8 9 10 11 12

13

14

21 20 19 18 17 16 15

22

23 24 25 26 27 28 29 30

Write the missing number.

29 _____ 31

Name _____

Draw a path inside each number.

21	22
23	24
25	26
27	28
29	30

Name

Connect the numbers **21-30** to make a picture. Color the picture.

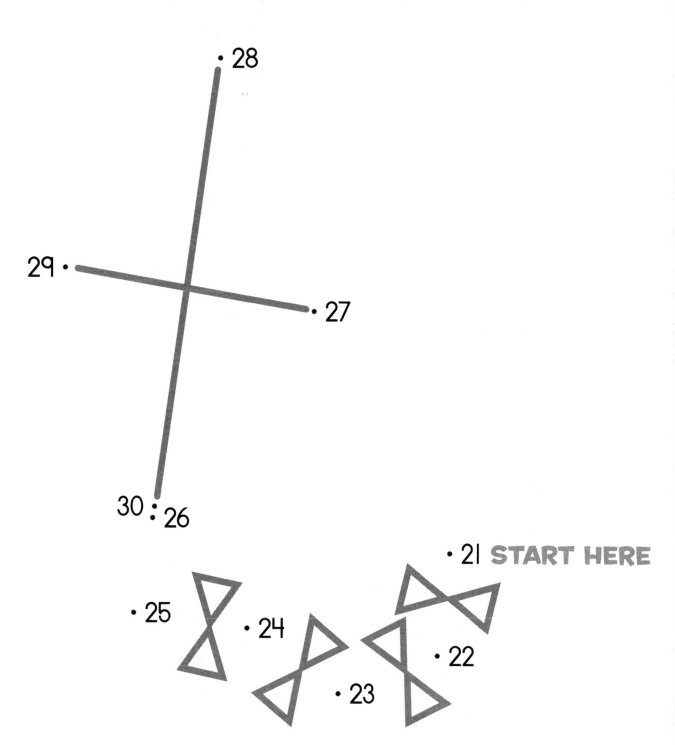

· 28

29 ·

· 27

30 · 26

· 21 **START HERE**

· 25

· 24

· 22

· 23

Name _____

Connect the numbers 1–30 to make a picture. Color the picture.

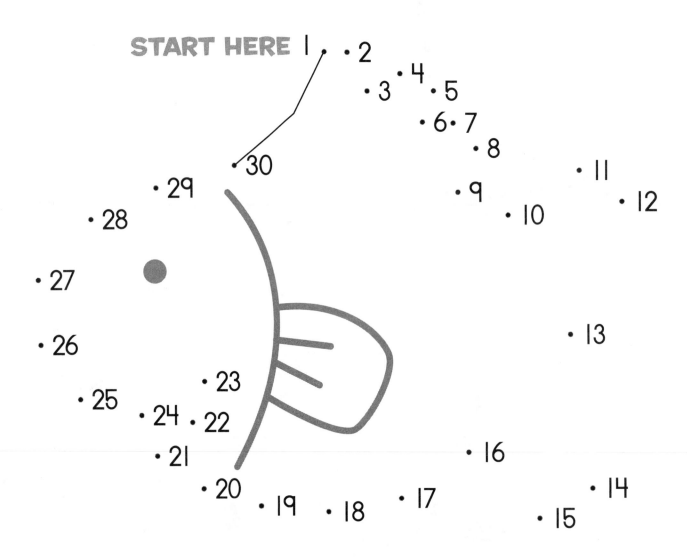

START HERE

Name _____

Fill in the missing numbers.

	2	3	4	
6	7	8	9	
11	12		14	15
16	17	18	19	20
21	22	23		25
	27	28	29	30

Name _____

100 one hundred

Draw a path inside the numbers.

Color each sun with a 100.

Name _____

100 one hundred

Draw 11 more suns to make 100.

Write the missing number.

 99 _____  101

ANSWER KEY

Page 6

Page 7

Color each crab with the number 1.

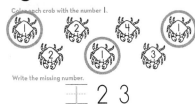

Write the missing number.

1 2 3

Page 8

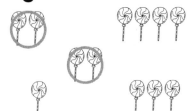

Page 9

Color each lollipop with the number 2.

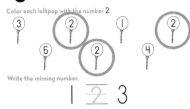

Write the missing number.

1 2 3

Page 10

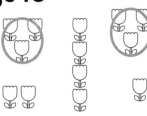

Page 11

Color each flower with the number 3.

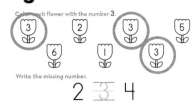

Write the missing number.

2 3 4

Page 12

Page 13

Color each banana with the number 4.

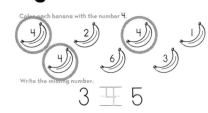

Write the missing number.

3 4 5

Page 14

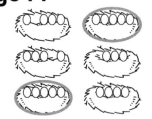

Page 15

Color each egg with the number 5.

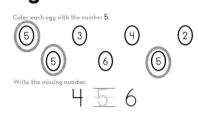

Write the missing number.

4 5 6

Page 16

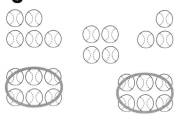

Page 17

Color each ball with the number 6.

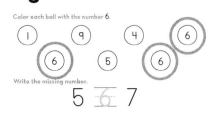

Write the missing number.

5 6 7

Page 18

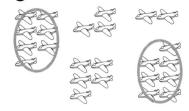

Page 19

Color each plane with the number 7.

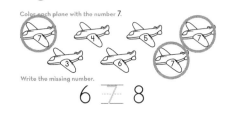

Write the missing number.

6 7 8

Page 20

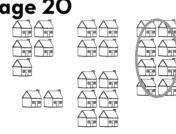

Page 21
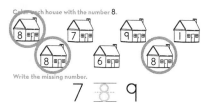

Page 22
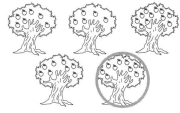

Page 23
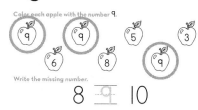

Page 24
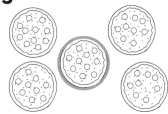

Page 25
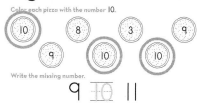

Page 27
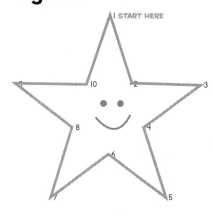

Page 28

Page 29
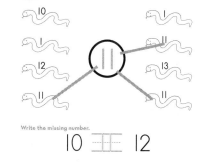

Page 30
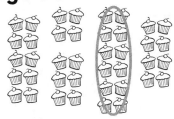

Page 31
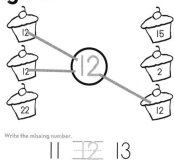

Page 32

Page 33
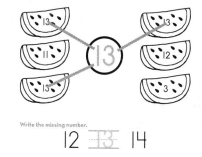

Page 34

ANSWER KEY

Page 35

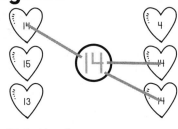

Write the missing number.
13 14 15

Page 36

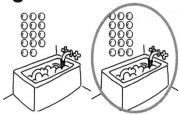

Page 37

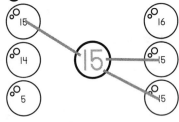

Write the missing number.
14 15 16

Page 38

Page 39

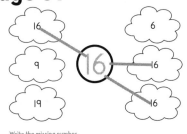

Write the missing number.
15 16 17

Page 40

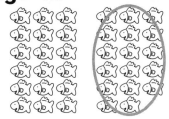

Page 41

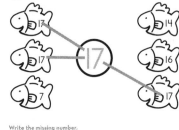

Write the missing number.
16 17 18

Page 42

Page 43

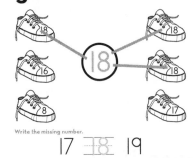

Write the missing number.
17 18 19

Page 44

Page 45

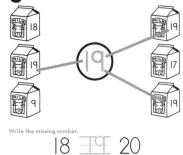

Write the missing number.
18 19 20

Page 46

Page 47

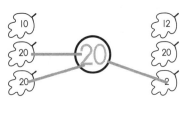

Write the missing number.
19 20 21

Page 49

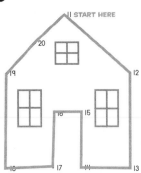

ANSWER KEY

Page 51

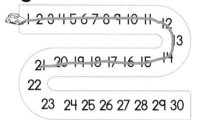

Write the missing number.

20 21 22

Page 53

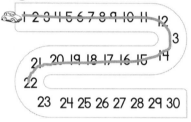

Write the missing number.

21 22 23

Page 55

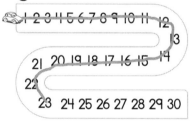

Write the missing number.

22 23 24

Page 57

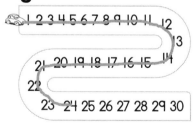

Write the missing number.

23 24 25

Page 59

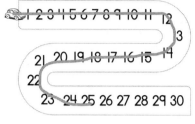

Write the missing number.

24 25 26

Page 61

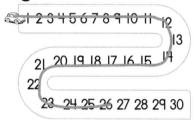

Write the missing number.

25 26 27

Page 63

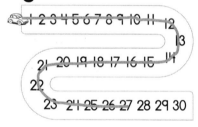

Write the missing number.

26 27 28

Page 65

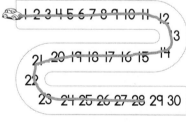

Write the missing number.

27 28 29

Page 67

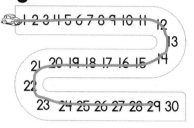

Write the missing number.

28 29 30

Page 69

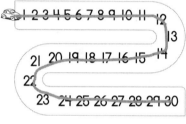

Write the missing number.

29 30 31

Page 71

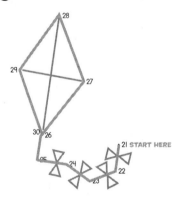

Page 72

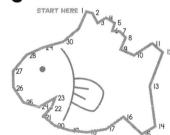